I0467897

Launch a Professional Looking Business in 48 Hours

-For Less Than 120 Bucks

By: Zechariah Blanchard

This book is dedicated to all the serial entrepreneurs out there that go from one business startup to another.

I would also like to thank all the mentors I have had in my life. They helped me learn all the things I know now about business.

Change a life: Be a mentor.

If you enjoy this book, please take the time to rate and review it online. Book sales rely very heavily on reviews.

If you thought this book could be better, I would love to hear from you! Email me at books@zechariahblanchard.com

Go to my website and subscribe to my newsletter to find out when I run promotions.

http://www.zechariahblanchard.com/

Table of Contents

Preface

Launching a business with a professional image doesn't have to take a long time. Now, you'll be able to do it in less than 48 hours. There are so many things you have to do to launch a business. It can seem like a daunting task, but it isn't anymore.

I have started more businesses than I can remember. Usually, the image of the business needs to become branded – virtually - overnight. In the entrepreneurial world, time is not just money, but it is what makes businesses rise and fall. I have spent such a significant chunk of time starting new businesses that I have gained a method for getting it done in record time for less than 120 dollars.

You might be asking yourself: How can I have a professional looking business in less than 48 hours with marketing materials, phone number, physical address, and things like uniforms? Well, that isn't all we are going to accomplish in less than 48 hours with a budget of 120 dollars or less. You will be walked through a myriad of different things that make your company look professional. The best part, they don't have to cost a fortune.

By the end of this book you will have everything your organization needs to project the appearance of a long standing professional company. You could utilize this book to give your current company a makeover in under 48 hours or to start a completely new business; the choice is yours. Whatever the reason is to use this book, it can do a tremendous amount for you in a very short period of time. Don't stop reading now and miss your opportunity to shine at your next company appearance.

Introduction

In the following pages you will learn about how to create the professional image for your business in less than 48 hours. All this for less than $120! Some of the things we will discuss include licensing, marketing materials and image, and different types of contact information. The list is long, but I have crammed it here for you to get through in record time. There are also links to online providers of most of the things you need. Some may require individual work.

Bonus Material:

Licensing is something most people get completely lost trying to accomplish. Not only is it almost impossible to figure out what licensing we need for a business, but we have to do it at 3 different levels of government or more. Learn ways to make this a relatively quick and painless process. There are simple techniques you can use to find what you need and how to get it in less than 48 hours.

One of the things we will focus on the most here is the image. Image is what really gives the impression of a professional company. If your organizational image is not professional in nature, people won't take your business seriously. Things like business cards, a website, brochures, product fliers and cards, signs, letterhead, vinyl wrap for your car, and even company uniforms can all be acquired for fewer than 120 dollars. Not to mention, you can do all this in less than 48 hours; sometimes less than 24 hours. All it takes is the knowledge of how to get it done right away.

Let's not forget about contact information to put on those cards, brochures, and giveaways. You need a way for people to fax you, phone you, email you, and send you letters and packages in the mail. You should also have a basic website with contact information, contact forms, and data procurement for collection of a customer list for future contact.

All these things and more are found inside this book. You should be able to read through this book and do one thing at a time. This will help you get everything done in time. If there is something you don't need for your business in particular you can forgo it and move on to another form of image creation. Don't let that big deal or event slip through your hands because of the image your company portrays to the potential client.

Get a folder for business documents and label it "New Business Documents." This is where we are going to keep all legal documents. It should be in a fire-safe filing cabinet or box.

If subheadings are listed with a time in parentheses, this is to reference how long it could take to complete. If you play your cards right, you will be done much faster.

Bonus Material: Licensing

Licensing requirements vary by state and local municipality. You are going to have to apply for licensing at three or more different branches of government. The first one I always apply for is the FEID from the IRS. Then, I move on to applying for state level licensing. After that, I move on to local county licensing. Last in the form of government is city licensing. You may also be under contract with a homeowners association. Each form of government will have to be contacted. These things can be done in one day.

Federal Licensing (10-15 min. online):

You should start your journey at the IRS website. Apply for an FEID online here: http://www.irs.gov/ just click on or search for "Apply for an Employer ID Number". At the time of this writing they only issued FEID numbers during business hours. The business hours listed at the time of this book are: Monday through Friday 7:00a.m. to 10:00p.m. Eastern Time. During business hours the process is quite straightforward. You will be asked a few questions about the business you are or have started. Once you are done you will get an FEID. Mine have been instant in the past. Print your FEID and place it in the "New Business Documents" folder.

State Licensing (1-2 hours online):

Now that you have your FEID you can move on to state licensing. The state level is where you will acquire your business entity status. Basically, you will file with the state to start a corporation, sole proprietorship, partnership, or some other form provided by your state. The type of business form you want depends on a few factors. Here are a few things that will help you decide on the type of business you want.

Sole Proprietorship – There is no business entity in essence. Everything belongs to you and you hold all the liability for the business. Not a good idea for a lot of businesses.

Partnerships – These are often a lot like sole proprietorships, but split up in different ways legally and financially. They have many different forms which vary by state.

Cooperative – The main goal of this type of organization is to meet the needs of a group of people. Every member pays in to the entity and benefits from it. This is usually small and local non-profit type groups.

Limited Liability Company – The basic idea here is to offer you the protections of a full blown corporation with the tax benefits of a sole proprietorship or partnership.

S-Corporation – Like a C-Corporation but taxed only on the personal level.

C-Corporation – Full blown corporation that requires meetings to take place and paperwork to be filed yearly. This is generally good for larger companies.

Lookup your state website on the United States Small Business Administration website at this link: http://www.sba.gov/licenses-and-permits.

Once you have decided on what the business structure you want is, call or go online with your state and apply for your licenses. Most states charge a small fee for these licenses. I print out a copy of my licenses right away if possible. Sometimes you have to wait for the actual license in the mail, other times you may be able to print it. No matter, you definitely need to print the license numbers or whatever you can get along with receipts and place them in your "New Business Documents" folder.

Make sure if there are any special regulatory agencies that you contact them about licensing requirements in your industry for your business.

County Licensing (1-2 hours in person):

The county licensing can usually be done at the county courthouse. Call ahead of time to find out where the licensing department is located, what the best time to come in is, and if you can make an appointment. Most of the time this will involve a few runs from one department to another and end with you leaving - licenses in hand. Prepare to spend a long time waiting. This is the reason you need to call ahead. You must squeeze every moment out your 48 hours to get everything done on time.

City Licensing (1-2 hours in person):

After you acquire the county licenses you will need to go to the city to find out about licensing in the city. If you don't live in the city this is unnecessary for you to do, unless you will operate your business in the city. City licenses can be the biggest pain because they sometimes hold the most stringent requirements.

Homeowners Association (0-1 hour):

These associations can have their own rules and regulations. Before you sign up for a business in your home (if that is legal where you live) you should contact your homeowners association to find out if there is anything special you need to do with them.

Licenses are required for you to do things like open a bank account, hire employees, charge customers, collect taxes, and prove you meet industry standards for regulated industries. Without them you can be dead in the water. Make sure you have the right licenses for your business.

Contact Information

Without contact information you won't be able to get reached by potential customers. Make sure you have a minimum of phone, fax, and email. Physical mailing address is also a nice thing to have, but not required. Your contact information will go on your licensing documents and all of your marketing materials. There are great sources for most of these requirements online.

Online Phone (15 minutes):

You can get several different types of online phone service but I prefer to use http://www.google.com/voice/ because it allows me to transfer a call directly to another phone. My new business number can be automatically ported to my current cellular phone. Google voice service is also free to use for the basics. I have never spent a dime on google.com/voice and I have used it for most business startups than I can think.

There are other online phone servers that give you a free number, but this is the best I have found. If you know of a better one, let me know!

Online Fax (10 minutes):
Not all businesses these days use a fax machine, but it does help with the professional image to have a fax number. There are two fax companies I use for my online faxing services. I like to use http://www.faxzero.com/ and http://www.k7.net/.

Faxzero.com offer free outbound faxes up to a certain number of pages. They place adds on the cover page for the free service, or you can pay a small fee and fax without ads. I have never heard a complaint about the fax with ads, but when I am sending a document to a client I always pay the fee to remove the ads.

K7.net is an online fax, phone, and message receiving service. They send the files directly to your email. The best part is their service is completely free! Your faxes get turned into a PDF file and emailed to you. Phone messages are also emailed to you, but I prefer to use google.com/voice for actual calls. You need to use the K7.net fax number at least once every few weeks or they will cancel your account. One way to do this is to send yourself a free fax from faxzero.com.

Email Address (10 minutes):

The email address should come directly from your domain name. If you have exampledomain.com then your email address should be YourName@exampledomain.com. This is something that will come after you create your DreamHost (Promo Code: BUSIN48) account and pick a domain name. Within your server/website control panel is a link on the upper left that says "manage email." Click that link.

Next, you want to click on "Create New E-mail Address," select the domain you want the email to be from, write YourName before the @ symbol, scroll down to where it says "List all e-mail addresses to forward to," and list an email address you check all the time as the forward to email.

I forward to my gmail.com account because they allow me to reply to emails as the account that was forwarded in. This way people see the email address they sent an email to in the reply instead of a reply from a random gmail.com address.

Mailing Address (1 hour):

This is not a requirement for a business to appear professional at first. You can always use your home address, but write it to the business at your address. Still, some people would like to have a physical address for their business in the first 48 hours. Here is how you can do it.

The United States Postal Service offers P.O. Boxes for relatively inexpensive. They are even cheaper at seldom traveled offices. You can order a P.O. Box online at: https://www.usps.com/business/get-a-po-box.htm/ by clicking "Reserve a PO Box" and filling out the information. PO Boxes start around fifteen bucks and go up from there. The price depends more on location than anything.

You also have the option of obtaining a real physical address for your mail. The United Parcel Service (UPS) offers physical locations in their stores. You can locate one locally by checking this link, http://www.theupsstore.com/mailboxes/Pages/index.aspx/ and clicking on "Find a Location." You will be directed to a map to locate a UPS store that offers mailbox services.

UPS requires that you go in to the store to get a mailbox. The prices vary widely by area and are usually quite a bit higher than USPS Boxes.

Clothing

One of the first things someone meeting you for business will see is your attire. Most professional businesses have company uniforms unless the employee wears a suit. Even then, most companies have a dress code. We are going to quickly go over how you can acquire custom embroidered clothes in less than 48 hours. Don't forget, it has to fall under our budget too.

Embroidered Shirt (2-3 hours):

First thing you need to do is locate a local embroiderer. I like to use a website like http://www.craigslist.org/ to find someone locally (you can also use the phonebook or web service like http://www.maps.google.com/). Spend about 20 minutes calling a few places for price quotes. You are looking to spend as little as possible and get it done immediately.

Be specific when you call, "I need to have a company name embroidered on two shirts and I need it right away. How long would it take you and how much would it cost?" You may also need to know the number of letters in the embroidered area. Target for this task is less than 10 bucks.

Make sure they know you are offering repeat business in the future.

After finding the place you are going to use, go to the nearest discount clothing retailer and pick up a new shirt for yourself. It should represent the business in a professional manner. Color choice is important. I recommend you choose some type of dark blue, preferably navy blue. Make sure to keep the price under eight bucks (go with what you think will work best with your target audience). I usually go with 3 button polo shirt with a collar. They look professional and are relatively inexpensive.

After you get the shirt head over to the embroiderer and have the shirt made with your company name. We are going to call this a total cost of $20.00 for a custom shirt made the same day.

You may have a shirt lying around the house you can use to have embroidered. That is all the better because the more money you save the lower the total budget has to be. I have tons of old business shirts in my closet. I use some of them for rags now when I work in the yard.

Marketing Materials

If you want to have a professional image you are going to need some marketing materials. You may be thinking, "Oh no! Where am I going to get those on such short notice?" Well, it isn't as hard as you think. I can have 50 business cards, ten brochures, 50 fliers, and a sign for less than fifty bucks. And, it can be done in one day or less. This requires you to have a minor amount of computer skill. Most of the work will be done for you.

We are going to download a few templates for marketing materials like: business cards, brochures, and fliers. We will also create a sign for printing when we get everything else printed.

Call around on a website like http://www.craigslist.org/ or look for printing businesses in the local area on a website service like http://www.maps.google.com/. You want someone that will print your materials immediately and not charge you a fortune. It is also important that they can cut the papers in the store. I have found that a lot of major chain retailers with print shops inside them are good about making a few prints and not breaking the budget.

Ask about pricing and file format requirements before you spend the time preparing everything and going to the store. Calling before you go can save a lot of time!

Usually, I am looking to spend less than a dollar per double-sided brochure in full color. No more than ten bucks for 10.

Business cards should be done the same way and should cost less than ten dollars. You need only to print ten sheets of cards on cardstock and have them cut the cards out using a bundle paper cutter.

Fliers should be printed on regular or color paper and should cost around fifteen cents each. You will print about 50 of these for less than ten bucks.

Your sign will likely be charged by the square foot. That means you need to keep the footage down to keep the cost down. Try to keep the sign cost down below twenty dollars.

Cards (15 minutes):

Download a card template for whatever word processing program you have. If you don't have one, or the one you own doesn't offer you templates from the internet, download LibreOffice (http://www.libreoffice.org/) or another open source office suite. Most office suite programs have a template search function. We are going to use it to find a business-card template.

If you can't find your templates, try looking under "create new file" or some other similar button. Usually the templates are hiding there.

Once you have located and downloaded a template, all you have to do is fill it in with your company information. Make sure the cut lines are printable on this document. The people at your local print shop are going to need to know where to cut the cards. Still, this should be relatively straightforward. After you are done, save the file in a folder marked "Print."

Brochure (30 minutes):

We are going to do basically the same thing for brochures as we did for cards. Locate a double sided brochure template which looks professional. Download the template and begin filling information into the brochure about your business.

Write information that makes you look more professional. You want the brochure to convey confidence. Don't lie, but let the positives shine through. What does your company do? Who is your customer base? Do a frequently asked questions section about your business.

It isn't hard to fill in a brochure for your company. This shouldn't take very long to do. Once you have both sides of the brochure done, save it inside the "Print" folder.

Fliers (30 minutes):

You can make fliers from a template or you can write your own. There is no special way they have to look. Fliers are one of my favorite marketing materials. They are easy to make, they look professional, and they are super cheap to print.

I'll assume you downloaded a template. Now, make two or three different fliers for your business. They can have pictures and limited text information. Even though this is all about image, remember, they might read what you wrote; it has to make sense and it should make your company look good.

Borders look great on fliers. Make them black and white to save money. It should go without saying, but they should be 8.5" x 11" if you want one per page. This is the easiest way to do fliers in my experience. When you are done, save each separate copy under a different name in the "Print" folder.

Sign (30 minutes):

The sign cost is going to depend on what size you need and what material it is made out of. I like to go with a sign about three feet across and one to two feet high. This makes the sign big enough to look serious, but small enough to be inexpensive. Normally, I advise using the cheapest material that won't fall apart on you. If you plan to use this for longer: go with something more expensive. You should be aiming for less than twenty dollars

There won't be a template for this, so we are going to have to make one. Most office suites give you the ability to expand the size of the page you are working with. You can expand your page to the size of your sign, zoom out, and create your sign, or you can use a presentation program that also comes with most office suites. The important thing is you end with a file you can use to make a sign.

Make sure if you use images on your sign that they are high resolution.

When you are done making your sign, save a copy in whatever format your printer uses and put it in the "Print" folder.

Printing (1-2 hours):

Make sure all your files are saved in a format the printer said they need. Then, load the files on a storage drive or email them directly to your printer. I prefer emailing the files directly before I leave. This way, if there is a problem with one of the files, they can tell me to fix it before I leave.

Try and find a printer that can do everyone at once, has a good price overall, and sounds like they know what they are doing. You can spend hours on end at a novice printer trying to get a file to print correctly. The printer should quickly provide you with high quality materials.

Find the person you spoke on the phone with when you get there. They can help you get in and out, fast. Have the prices they quoted you written down. Always ask for one proof print (the only exception is the sign). Tell them exactly what you are using each piece for. Explain how happy you are that they could get this all done for you today. Don't underestimate what a little kindness can do for you.

The right printing stock (paper or other material) is imperative in having everything come out right. Ask the advice of the employee to find a good material to use for your stuff. Always use a heavy cardstock for the business cards.

Make sure the printer cuts the cards to the right size. Don't pay for something that doesn't come out right.

You can also print some of these things at home with materials you already have. The cost is high in ink, but it's fast and convenient.

Website

Any professional business today has a website. If you don't have a basic website to put on your cards and materials, it is going to be much harder to convince people you are serious. You will also want to have your email address: FirstName@YourSite.com because it increases credibility. That is really what we are working on here: credibility. You might not think you can have a website overnight, but you can. You are going to have a website, fully hosted, auto-installed, and ready to get updated by you in no time.

Server, Domain, & Website (1-2 hours):

First thing you are going to do is acquire a server and domain name. I have created a special deal for you on DreamHost. You can click that link or go to http://www.dreamhost.com and enter the promo code: BUSIN48 and you will get one year of virtual server hosting with a free domain. This is a coupon code for **$75.00 off** a year of hosting *and* **a free domain**. You can make this domain whatever you want that is available. It can be automatically hosted on DreamHost with the click of a button during checkout.

Your domain name is important. It should be short, concise, and tell everyone who you are. Consider how it will look on marketing material.

Go to that link or use that code and pick a website address for your business. Try to make it small. The name of the business, or a shortened version people would recognize. Consider what it will look like on a business card and other marketing material. Think about how someone typing an email to FirstName@yournewwebsitegoeshere.com will feel when they have to remember it, type it, or write it down. This website is your company brand. Make it a good choice.

Once you have picked your web address, make sure you select fully host this domain now or something like that. This will host the domain for you so you can auto install. This is one of the things I really like about them. In the DreamHost panel, within the top left box, it says "one-click-installs." Click that section. Find WordPress and select custom installation. Make sure it installs to your website and automatically creates a database. Click "install it for me now." They will install it and email you when it is ready for the next step (very quickly).

You will receive an email that tells you what to do to finish installing your website. Follow the directions. WordPress is very easy to use and there is an enormous community out there for support. There are a lot of free templates in WordPress that change the entire appearance of the website at the click of a button. Find a theme (as they are called) and customize it over the course of a few hours. Start with something very basic that only requires a little text editing. When you create a page, fill it with content and move on to the next page.

Some pages you might want to include are: About Us, Careers, Recent Developments, The Team, and Contact Us. At the very least you should have a contact page, about page, and an article about the company on the home page. It has to have elements of a fully functioning website. This is all about image. People are more likely to search for information about you online than to ask you in person.

WordPress has an amazing online community. You can find the main page at: http://www.wordpress.org/ or the support forums at: http://www.wordpress.org/support/. The themes you can install from WordPress are often supported by the creator in the WordPress forums.

Email Signup Link (1 hour):

It is good to have an email signup link on your website's main page. I like to use a service like http://www.mailchimp.com/ because they are free for small to medium list sizes, have a great website based email builder, provide you with all code and links for your signup form, and rarely end up in the spam folder.

Once you have created the account you need to create a list for people to be added to. Then, go to your admin panel in WordPress and click on plugins. Search for MailChimp, install the plugin, link your account to the plugin, and put it on your site to start collecting emails.

Overall, mailchimp.com is a great business tool to make you look and feel more professional. Also, having an email list also makes you appear to be a longer standing company. No one knows how many people are on your list.

You are judged by the image you portray everyday. Make yours count.

Video on Homepage (1-2 hours):

It can make you look more professional if you have a video on your homepage. The video should be in relatively descent quality, but doesn't have to be professionally done. Though, you can sometimes find students to make professional videos for little to nothing. It helps them with their credits and experience, and gives you a semi-professional video free of charge.

The video can be made using a movie maker on your computer. Keep the editing simple and just cut from one scene to another. Make the video between one and three minutes so you have time to do it and have enough to say. This timeframe will also help you keep the attention of your audience. You should include a little about your company, what you are doing, where you are going, and who you are in the video.

Record the video, edit it at home, and upload it to a website like http://www.youtube.com/. YouTube requires a google account for uploading, but makes the process extremely easy for you. Add a few tags in there and upload the video. After the video is done processing YouTube will provide you with a code to embed the video in your website. All you have to do is click on embed video or share this video. Then, highlight the code, copy it, and paste it into your website.

Free Press Releases

Nothing says professional like a google.com or bing.com search that turns up a bunch of press releases about your company. There are tons of free press release sites out there, but most of them won't get you very far. I have quite a bit of experience with press releases. Here are a few of my favorite sites for freebie releases:

Paid press releases have their place when you are announcing big news and want it to go out to a national audience, but most things can be solved with a few free releases.

PRLog:

http://www.prlog.or/ is a great site that offers a free press release. Their release goes out virtually immediately, has a ton of features, and becomes indexed in google.com, bing.com, yahoo.com and other major search engines extremely fast. This provides top page rank in search engines for your release. They also offer clickable links for you to add clout to your new website.

Free Press Release:

http://www.free-press-release.com/ is another good site for free press releases. They offer a permanent place on their site, quality SEO, and indexing on major search engines. The upgraded releases are much better, but the free one offers quite a bit.

PRUrgent:

http://www.prurgent.com/ is one of my favorites because it distributes free releases to news sites like news.google.com. They are a little pickier than some of the other sites, but the results are worth the time. Create an account and submit a free release to them. Pay a nominal free and the release will be sped through the system and placed at the top of other releases.

National Public Radio/TV:

http://www.npr.org/ is where you can submit your release directly to any show from NPR radio or TV. This is nice for when you know who the exact audience is you are trying to get in touch with. Their submission is super simple too. You use the contact form and select press release submission. Then pick the show you want the release to go to.

24/7 Press Release:

http://www.24-7pressrelease.com/ - almost didn't make my list because they don't send out your release when it is free. Still, they index fast on major search engines and it can't possibly hurt you to submit a release on their page.

Writing a Press Release:

Press releases must be written in the third person as a news story. Titles should be catchy and draw people in. The subtitle should give a two to three sentence summary of the article. There should be a "boiler" at the bottom of the release that gives your contact information and key information about your company.

You need to make sure your press release is unique to each site you send it to. The header should grab the attention of the reader. Check out a few of these articles to write your first rock solid press release. Most of these articles offer templates. If your press release is not in the right format it won't be accepted by anyone, let alone a free release site.

http://www.wikihow.com/Write-a-Press-Release

http://blog.hubspot.com/marketing/press-release-template-ht

http://www.entrepreneur.com/article/226011

http://www.huffingtonpost.com/zach-cutler/press-release-tips_b_2120630.html

Work Schedule and Costs

If you want to get everything done in a two day time-frame, make sure you follow this guide or one just like it that you make for yourself. There is a lot of wasted time in doing anything with a business. You need to eliminate as much of the waste as possible to get this done in 48 hours or less.

The assumption here is that you are going to be spending two straight days working on this project, and they are going to be business days. I assume business hours are going to be between 8AM and 8PM. So, technically, we are launching this professional business in 24 hours!

Here are the tasks we need to accomplish:
Licensing
Clothing
Marketing Materials
Website
Contact Information
Spreading the Word (Press Releases)

Day 1	
8:00–8:59AM	Call state and local agencies to find out what licenses are required for your business.
9:00-10:59AM	File paperwork for required licenses with the federal, state, and local government.

11:00-11:59AM	Call around and locate someone to embroider a shirt for you and also a place to get a mailing address (PO Box or Physical address).
12:00-12:59PM	Take Lunch
1:00-2:59PM	Go get shirt embroidered and acquire the mailing address.
3:00-3:59PM	Find a print services company that can print your files tomorrow. Make sure you know what format they require.
4:00-4:59PM	Acquire an online fax number and phone number.
5:00-8:00PM	Signup for web hosting and domain name through DreamHost. Install WordPress, install a custom theme, and make an email address at your domain.

Day 2	
8:00-9:59AM	Download templates and create marketing materials for printer.
10:00-11:59AM	Get marketing materials printed.
12:00-12:59PM	Lunch
1:00-8:00PM	Customize your website, write a press release, add MailChimp signup, and complete other tasks that have not been complete.

Total Costs

Licensing: Depends on Location
Clothing: $20.00
Website, hosting, & Email: $45.00
Brochures: $10.00
Cards: $10.00
Fliers: $10.00
Sign: $20.00
Phone: $0.00
Fax: $0.00
Email: $0.00
Press Release Marketing: $0.00
Homepage Video: $0.00

Total Cost: $115.00

|

Note to Readers

I hope you enjoyed the book. I love writing, and I really love business. I have been launching business ventures since I was in elementary school. I have a real passion for sharing my knowledge with other people.

If you have any comments, I love hearing from readers. Just email me at books@zechariahblanchard.com or find me on facebook, twitter, or linedin.

I am available for consulting, speaking engagements, and training. Please contact me via my website for more information.

How can I make this book better? If you don't think my book is worth 5 stars I want to know why. Shoot me over an email. If you think it is worth 5 stars then don't forget to head over to Amazon and review it now. Thanks!!!

Sincerely,
Zechariah Blanchard

Like the book?

If you enjoyed the book and thought it was a good value for the cost, leave a review. It means a lot to me when I get the chance to read what someone thought about my book and reviews are the lifeblood of sales.

Thanks for reading and reviewing!

Contact me with any questions:
books@zechariahblanchard.com

Other books by Zechariah Blanchard
Leading the Curve

How Key Leaders Get on Top and Stay There

LEADING
THE
CURVE

**Maximize the Efficiency,
Productivity, and Adaptability
of Your Business**

Zechariah Blanchard

Author of Creativity, Innovation, and Entrepreneurship

Leading the Curve
Maximize the Efficiency, Productivity, and
Adaptability of Your Business

By Zechariah Blanchard

Ever wonder how market leaders get to the top and stay there? Now, you can take a step in the right direction by moving to the front of your industry. Leading the Curve is how you are going to get there. The author walks the reader through different principles of leadership that market-leaders are using today.

Written in a conversational-tone, the book walks the reader through what they can do to start leading their industry, right now. You won't be sorry you downloaded this e-book. From leading by example all the way to teamwork development, there is something for leaders at every level of organization.

The world is ever changing and you need an edge. Without something to set you apart, your organization and position are going to become obsolete. Leading the Curve will give you the edge you need to start leading your people to victory. Your workplace will become more efficient, more productive, and more adaptable to situations.

Pick up your copy and start leading your industry today!

51

Saltwater Fish and Reef Tanks

Saltwater Fish and Reef Tanks
From Beginner to Expert

By Zechariah Blanchard

<u>Saltwater Fish and Reef Tanks</u> is a great book for the beginner saltwater hobbyist – or anyone that wants to know the easy way to own and maintain a quality saltwater reef tank.

Zechariah was the managing owner of a small saltwater aquarium store in Orlando, FL. While working in the store he helped hundreds of customers solve problems with their aquariums ranging from beginner to expert.

His book about reef aquariums is directed toward the person who wishes to learn a considerable amount of information from one location. He discusses purchase, setup, cycling, buying livestock, caring for your inhabitants, and a whole lot more!

You can find <u>Saltwater Fish and Reef Tanks</u> available in Kindle and paperback form on Amazon.com and at other major retailers. Get your copy right now!

Creativity, Innovation, and Entrepreneurship
Keys to the Future of Human Society

By Zechariah Blanchard
Copyright ©2010 Zechariah Blanchard

Creativity, Innovation, and Entrepreneurship dives into which aspects of business and society bring about the changes we love and need to move forward. Zechariah breaks down and explains creativity, innovation, and entrepreneurship in a way that is easy to understand.

He offers the reader examples and analogies to help better explain how these things play a crucial role in the future of our society.

The author believes that creativity, innovation, and entrepreneurship have played an imperative role in the past, present, and will continue to play an imperative role in the future.

Mr. Blanchard explores many different areas of creativity, innovation, and entrepreneurship. He also goes into detail about how they can be applied to individuals and groups.

Creativity, Innovation, and Entrepreneurship is available in electronic and paperback form on Amazon.com and at other major retailers. Get your copy right now!

Speaking Engagements and Training

Zechariah Blanchard is available for speaking engagements within the United States.

Mr. Blanchard can speak on any of the topics from this book or his other books.

He also offers training seminars that start at a few hours and can last as long as several days.

You can contact him about the details of a speaking engagement via his website: www.ZechariahBlanchard.com

You can also contact the author on facebook, twitter, and linkedin.

Send paper correspondence to:

Zechariah Blanchard
PO Box 677413,
Orlando, FL 32867

About the Author

 Zechariah Blanchard holds a Bachelors of Science in Business Management – Entrepreneurship from the University of Central Florida. He has worked in management at the corporate and entrepreneurial level.

Mr. Blanchard believes entrepreneurship will usher in the future of our society. He has learned the importance of launching a professional looking campaign – rapidly - in the entrepreneurial-world. He enjoys passing his knowledge and passion along to other leaders and entrepreneurs.

For more information about Zechariah Blanchard, check out his website: http://www.zechariahblanchard.com

He can also be found on facebook, twitter, linkedin, and by searching for him online.

Mr. Blanchard is a disruptive Entrepreneur. He enjoys entering markets where there is room for rapid advancement and improvement on the current business climate.

Contact Zechariah at
ZJamesBlanchard@gmail.com